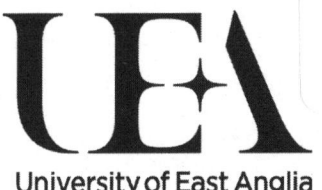

UEA
University of East Anglia

AF067281

Poets

Creative Writing Anthologies

2013

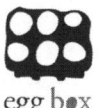

egg box

UEA 7 Poets 2013

First published by Egg Box Publishing 2013

International © 2013 retained by individual authors

This book is sold subject to the condition that it shall not, by way of trade or otherwise, be lent, resold, hired out, stored in a retrieval system, or otherwise circulated without the publisher's prior consent in any form of binding or cover other than that in which it is published and without a similar condition including this condition being imposed on the subsequent purchaser.

A CIP record for this book is available from the British Library.

UEA 7 POETS 2013 is typeset in 10pt Caslon with 13pt leading. Titles in Din, of various weights.

Printed and bound in the UK by Imprint Digital.

Designed and typeset by Sean Purdy.

Cover photography by Christopher Corby.

Proofread by Sarah Gooderson.

Distributed by Central Books.

ISBN: 9780957661110

Acknowledgements

Thanks are due to the School of Literature, Drama and Creative Writing at UEA in partnership with Egg Box Publishing for making this anthology possible.

We'd also like to thank the following people:

Moniza Alvi, Amit Chaudhuri, Andrew Cowan, William Fiennes, Giles Foden, Sarah Gooderson, Lavinia Greenlaw, Rachel Hore, Kathryn Hughes, Katie Konyn, Daniel Leeson, Michael Lengsfield, Jean McNeil, Natalie Mitchell, Beatrice Poubeau, Rob Ritchie, Michèle Roberts, James Scudamore, Ali Smith, Helen Smith, Henry Sutton, George Szirtes, Val Taylor, Steve Waters and Peter Womack.

Nathan Hamilton at Egg Box Publishing and Sean Purdy.

Editorial team:

Beatrice Armstrong
Krishan Coupland
Timothy Lawrence
Rachel Mendel
Matthew McGuinness
Faith Ng
Caroline Pearce
Lauren Rose
Naomi Spicer
Jo Surzyn
Laura Westerman

Contents

Introduction
George Szirtes — vii

Contributors
Martin Farrar — 1

Neil Gregory — 7

Jennifer Grey — 16

UEA Anthology 2013

....

Meghan Guss   —   23

Kim Lockwood   —   30

Jackie Martin   —   38

Kate Pannett   —   46

....

Introduction

George Szirtes

This will be my last contribution to such introductions as I am retiring at the end of the year after some twenty years of teaching poetry to those who want to write it. The last seven of those years have been spent very happily at UEA. I have been proud to be associated with such a renowned course and am delighted to introduce a selection of poems to compare with the best before.

The selection is as comparable as it is different, since every good poet has always been, and has to be, different. Some of our best poets have been lyrical, formalist, minimalist, philosophical. They have included outstanding writers of prose poetry. There is, as will be immediately apparent reading the contents of this book, no house style. Teaching is by intelligent, informed conversation, a natural collection of people sharing a passion in which understanding is as important as close textual criticism. Many students have gone on, in their different ways, to publish books and win prizes. But poetic development is a long-term business and all one year at an institution can do is to help set up the base camp from which to proceed through a lifetime.

Here then are some fine different base camps.

Martin Farrar's is an intensely humane poetry, focused on disturbance. His formal control of verse and pattern is highly sophisticated but his language is never formal. Those buildings with their 'unbreakable patience, large lovelessness' in *Big Buildings* are the bodies we grow among. The uncanny and tragic aspects of the everyday are his theme. 'The gut unknots / a hot wash of dinner' he writes in *The Liver*. There is real confidence and power in his poems. They treat of ordinary lives and resound through them.

Neil Gregory's work is marked by intelligence, often in a short narrative context. The emotional freight is not concentrated in specific lines but distilled through the whole. His voice comprises a wide range of influences and styles. The wit of *[untitled]* is one aspect of it, the view of catastrophe in *Space Jump* is another. Neil Gregory is, in himself, a highly gifted group of base camps of ideas and apprehensions moving into verse.

Jennifer Grey is different again. The poems present us with a mind excitingly packed with images and ideas that stretch the limits of poetry as verse. Her poetry lies in the sharp registering of dramatic fragments, as in *The Fifth Day* where a gull tries to pull its legs from the sea, and in a world where even your skin 'will begin to elude you' (*A Birthday Poem*). She invents neologisms such as 'catshape' for her *Apocalypse*. It is the jags and interrupted inches (*City Centre, Winter*) that matter.

There is a pulse of real energy in Meghan Guss's work. It comprises a personal blend of wit and passion. The poetic couples of Poet Lovers become more than a caricature of themselves, they are vivid commentaries on their own art. There is a sense of pressure throughout the poems. 'The machines are breathing' she says in *Drone*, and 'I misheard my / blood'. Thoughts like 'bloated zeppelins' in *Launch* convey the balance between humour and haunting.

Kim Lockwood's poems present us with an intensely rich, crystal-like aggregation of words around a core perception. The central persona is engaged with direct experience, the sense of being an identity entering a sensory and, at the same time, psychological space. It is like stepping into the swimming pool of *they were scared maybe the water will come up*. Like Gregory she deploys a range of approaches from prose poetry through line spaces of *LP*.

The world of Jackie Martin's poems is more social than either Gregory's or Lockwood's. Her subjects are observed as part of a tapestry of lives. She has an eye and ear for the suddenly fascinating detail like the 'shed-bound, peg-mouthed, crust-mucking' woman in *House On The Corner*. Her poems are close to colloquial speech, spiked with humour and the quirky pleasures of words. Hers is a constantly humane poetry.

The world of memory furnishes the moving vignettes of Kate Pannett. Clarity and precision are the key to the poems, the way a scene finds itself transformed from personal to universal almost without trying. This happens particularly in the shorter poems, like the sonnet-length *Bottom Drawer* where the suitcases and umbrella suddenly take on a poignant power, and in *Changing* with its 'women drying like washing'.

It is a privilege to have worked with such gifted, committed poets in the making. I hope to keep track of them as they move into lives beyond the course. Their progress beyond the base camp will require moments of good luck as does life generally. I wish them that luck, the fair gusts that help them over difficult, still or troubled moments. And I wish pleasure to the reader, a pleasure I am confident they will find in these pages.

....

George Szirtes
Reader in Creative Writing

UEA Anthology 2013

Martin Farrar

Driving
Big Buildings
Abort
The Liver
Variations on a Mistake
Not Cricket

Driving

I know I can't be driving the car.
This somehow involves my father's feet
and a black stick, but I go with it
as I sit in his lap and hold the wheel.

*

I'm seventeen and he won't let me do
anything he does twice as well.
On curves his firm hand brings me straight.
At each tight spot he backs me in.

*

I still suspect he held something back:
a secret pedal, an extra turn in the wheel.
I almost see him shaking his head
when I stall. This kid will never learn.

*

I'm being towed by a truck and a rope.
I steer my dead car through the streets
telling myself if I hold the wheel
someone will handle the rest.

Big Buildings

Town halls hunker forward on fat columns.
Stadiums cup their grass protectively.
Office blocks shoulder the sky to one side.

Old museums have hearts hung from ceilings
in squared-off, serene, symmetrical stone.
The new museums are curving tilting drunks.

In shopping centres bodies rise up
escalators, the walls are made of glass
and ownership is a kind of soft fudge.

Factories disassemble vacant space
behind gap-tooth windows, or they smoke pipes
and empty their bellies into long trucks.

Cathedrals are grey pyramids veined with scaffolding.
Cinemas are caverns of loud, bright thought.
Lighthouses are tower dreams, somewhere near the sea.

Big buildings. I spread my arms across
their wide, rough walls: impending scale,
unbreakable patience, large lovelessness.

Abort

I woke one morning from the strangest dream
and turned to tell it but my wife was gone,
her side of the bed a hot dip of creases.

*My dream: I woke reflected in the glass
of a pod door, and remembered who I was.
The cheering crowds, flash photographs, then space.
I was the last hope of a dying planet.*

Four years of marriage coursed through my veins
purging my dream but leaving its strange dread
of something lost or changed. When she came home

*The door slid back and an eight-year-old boy
held out his hand. There are new requirements
he explained, washing hypersleep from my skin,
and you're way off course. It's time to go home.*

she couldn't stop crying, and all at once I felt
the full weight of my prophetic omniscience.
It's over she said. There's nothing you can do.

*To what? I asked. The things I loved are gone.
All I have left... I turned to the dark void
still and lifeless beyond the ship's portholes.
Sorry said the child. It's out of my hands.*

At that moment all the airlocks opened
sucking the breath from my lungs. We drifted apart
through the airless house, bouncing off the walls.

The Liver

Give in, give it all back. The gut unknots
a hot wash of dinner, a milky broth
still redolent of wine, whisky and beer.
Say to the children stood at your back
      Go on, get out of here.

Don't guess what they divine in strings of spit,
a glistening web between the bowl and your lips,
the lips that say *be good* or *give me a kiss*,
lips speckled with your soft, pale flecks
      of human ambergris.

Place one hand on each side of the slippery rim
for the aftershock, the sweating and heaving.
Now spy in your buttery spew and spatter
the tinsel strands of red and black
      that speak of a darker matter.

Drop that thought off the steep cliff of your brain.
Tell the kids that you won't tell them again.
Stand up and gob, flush away the stain.
Your mind expels what it can't correct
      like water down a drain.

Turn around grinding a towel in your hands
to explain to the kids *You have to understand...*
but what can you say, there's nobody there.
Throw the towel back on its rack
      and bless the empty air.

Martin Farrar

Variations on a Mistake

As you sit down
I pull the chair from under you
but you don't see
and sit on air for several minutes,
my sweet naïf, my Wile E Coyote.

As you sit down
I pull the chair from under you
sliding in a smaller chair. Before you land
I replace it with an even smaller chair, then one smaller still,
in this way lowering you gently to the ground.

As you sit down
I pull the chair from under you
but I somehow see the fear in your eyes
and put it back. You'll never know
where you got that sense of falling.

As you sit down
I pull the chair from under you.
The restaurant chatter stops. Forks are suspended,
faces aghast. You stand into the silence, give them your winsome smile
and take a bow. The audience goes wild.

....

Martin Farrar was born in West Yorkshire and completed his BA and MA in Creative Writing at UEA. He loves big buildings.

Neil Gregory

Report on a Passing Glance
"and then, I hear it"
Deprivation Tank
[untitled]
Towards a Definition of Yesterday
Space Jump

Report on a Passing Glance

You couldn't say they met;
they just converged, were cut

a little slack by the universe,
which, ever the romantic, bent its own laws

and shrank the expanse between their lives
to a ratio of 0:0, let their worlds quantise

from analogues of sensation
to a point beyond the measure of spectrums.

The black holes in their heads
aligned, for all the space-time there is

between blinks, became a wormhole
leading nowhere but now, a portal

to an instant without history and future,
when they knew themselves, whoever

they might have been just then.

"and then, I hear it"

after William Stafford

Listen: it is your voice,
calling back and forward,
run into my head
by a digital stream
I'd like to imagine
you stooping over,
bleeding into.

It's just noise; there
are bones in me, trembling
under the weight
of your pebble cadences,
fracturing into phonemes
that clop and chew my senses
on dark nights and dark roads

when coyote yips
carry my throat
into unmarked distances
of fir tops, creaking
under new snow,
too raw for tyre tracks –
placeless, all-over sounds

falling and falling –
lifetimes of insects
stiffening in sharp
grass, canyons of bark,
the cleat treads
of stumbling feet
that grew lost.

Deprivation Tank

questions leave you stranded   dip your fingers   if you want to get the gist of refraction   to understand how light lies   immerse yourself in negative space   you'll feel your topography   recognise the elevation of your skin   you'll understand that depth   close your lids   needn't be charged with so much authority   you can't plumb the bed of a thought   can't measure the ends to its disturbances   it's the ping of a voice   push it from your head   it will chain-react   relocate itself in echoes   like you the ripples   stop and don't   memory's the same   breathe concentrics overlapping   interfering   rebounding through chambers   not so different   from the impact of a footstep   from insides bubbling to air   listen   there's been a change of current   you might be standing up   casting noise across the surface you might be inside-out   fathoms from home   for all you know   you are gravity

Neil Gregory

[untitled]

[1] Although the poem is untitled, earlier drafts carry the heading 'For the Trees' (See also note 9).

[2] The short lyric form of the poem is consistent with much of the poet's early work, but the use of syllabic metre is apparently anomalous.

[3] The close proximity of *treaty* and *fission* (division or splitting into parts) foreshadows the juxtaposition of urban constraint and natural freedom that permeates the poem through imagery such as the *boards* [...] *nailed // against our storm*.

[4] *Alleyed:* an invented verb construction of 'alley', meaning, presumably, 'to occupy a narrow space'; the similarity to 'allied' could also imply a state of unity in opposition to a common enemy or adversity of considerable force or scope.

[5] *nursing our red wings* may refer to 'Redwings' by the American poet, James Wright, a known influence.

[6] The play on the homophones 'creek' and 'creak' in *creek beds* further reinforces the urban/nature juxtaposition and evokes the near noiseless isolation of the speaker and his or her companion(s).

[7] *lachrymal bones,* which form part of the eye socket, are the smallest and most fragile bones on the human face; lachrymal (also 'lacrimal' or 'lacrymal') is connected with weeping or tears, and hence recalls the *leaking cliffs* of the third stanza.

⁸ *klaxons // pandemic:* by associating the klaxons – which could be police sirens – with a viral outbreak, this image appears to condemn social authority.

⁹ As stated in note 1, *For the Trees* appears in earlier drafts of the poem as a working title. Its relocation to the closing couplet has consequently led some critics to read the poem as being fundamentally concerned with the famous English language idiom 'can't see the wood for the trees'.

Towards a Definition of Yesterday

Where do I draw the line
in the last week of January?

Was it a Tuesday
between pivotal and commonplace?

Was it just another revolution
on the cryptic crossword?

Can it be measured by getting all the clues
of the Earth?

Should I put it down as the first snowfall of the year,
reheated for lunch and dinner?

Or leftover shepherd's pie,
whitening the tops of people's heads?

Was it the day I traced the outline of a camel
living 4000m above sea level in the mountains of Bhutan?

Or when I watched a television programme about tigers
in the frost on the rear window of the car?

Space Jump

He doesn't watch
the live stream,
just lies back,
the whole world
at his feet,
trying to make sense
of all the lights
he can't see.
At such altitude,
up and down
switch places.
A nod to posterity,
then the voice
of God, telling him
it's pancreatic –
and that's all
the sound that catches
as he drops,
from over 120,000 feet,
to the thinness
of a hospital mattress.

Neil Gregory has been exploring his own and others' work on the Poetry strand of the MA in Creative Writing. His work has appeared in *Writing Magazine*, *InTheRed Magazine*, and *Lung Jazz: Young British Poets for Oxfam* (Cinnamon Press and Eyewear Publishing, 2012).

Jennifer Grey

The Fifth Day
Reading Pascale Petit in a Power Cut
A Birthday Poem
Apocalypse in a Domestic Setting Fig No. 42
Thoughts on Narrowly Missing a Deer on an Unidentified East Anglian Backroad at 3AM
City Centre, Winter

The Fifth Day

The men were marching inland by the fourth day,
Teeth clenched against the cold, their palms red raw
From trying to unmoor the Fishboats anchored by the swell.
By morning only I was left.
                        I skate in and out from shore to improvise a tide,
Mounting the humpbacks of waves above the stares of fish. Their gills stand open,
As if they gasped when their oxygen began to cut like glass.
                        My father was the Fishman, once.
I tell them of his knife, describe it dancing over bellies 'til they flapped
Like empty nets caught in a breeze.
                        Beside his boat a gull crawks and croaks,
Churning rosy slush as it tries pulling its legs out of the sea.
I put one finger to the salt burred ground,
Testing for a thaw.

Reading Pascale Petit in a Power Cut

she reads poems about mandrakes by torchlight when the power cuts and thinks
this will never do

she turns the phones off takes the milk out of the fridge
drinks straight out of the carton counting raindrops
she wonders if there will be lightning she wonders if

a man in a lightning yellow mac will turn up with a clipboard to say
the power'll be back on soon they're just switching the rain off
any noises from the roof are just the boys catching raindrops
would you like a glass for that milk love?

if she was Pascale Petit she'd have sex with him on the sofa while every light in
the house blazed and then write lines about the milk of mandrakes running over
her lips while lightning struck the roof tiles and out in the hall the clipboard lay
abandoned on top of the poems

as it is he'll tick her name off his list and move on to the neighbours
to warn them about the council's new initiative
of forcing precipitation into cartons
so the street can go about its business undisturbed by lightning
or by poems that only stick in the throat
when read by torchlight

she puts the mandrakes in the fridge puts the milk on the bookshelf and thinks
what do I want this to do anyway

A Birthday Poem

On realising that after this:
Your skin will begin to elude you. Despite your pullings, pluckings, smoothings,
It will pucker off the bone, change shape when you haul it with both fingers,
Sag off your neck in wattles.

You will try to catch yourself by resting your nose in the crook of your arm, where
you used to catch your own scent uncurling from under the perfume you applied
each morning, smell only the sour musk of the last bottle you threw away.

On realising that after this:
Your eyes will become unfamiliar. You will catch yourself in the act of smiling
As you pass the bedroom mirror and jolt back from the gaudy ring of iris
Circling the dark gape of pupil.

You will dream that you are teetering on a precipice and half wake to find
your hands twitching, as if grasping the air could stop you falling through your
mattress, your heart creaking in your chest.

On realising that after this:
Your nails will have a yellow cast. You will start painting them peach
On the day the names on headstones become familiar ones,
On the day you find it colder than usual for spring.

Apocalypse in a Domestic Setting Fig No. 42

In this house, the ceilings crink to the press of footsteps. He swaggers on about the end of the world. She gets clagged up with beerswill to understand. She scratches a catshape on his baccy so she doesn't have to look at him. It grins at her. Yesterday, she blew smoke signals up the chimney to that upstairs flat. She thought maybe they'd save her. Or him. Now she thinks they should save cartooncat. She cracks a window, pokes the picture out. It flops to the ground, mouth triumph-wide. The shadow of his palm touches her before he does. She tries not to care.

Thoughts on Narrowly Missing a Deer on an Unidentified East Anglian Backroad at 3AM

As it swerves its eyes down one clean arc towards the bumper, I think I see
My father,
Sat beside a stage where guitarists play the tune we listened to
The night we drove the car
For miles along the backroads, turning up the volume 'til the drumbeat ticked
A metronome
By which I paced my breaths as we danced a slalom round the bends.
My father's hands
Beat the same three-four time that winds out of my speakers now as I pull
Sharply to the left
Then sit there for an hour, waiting for the song to stop pulsing through my chest.

Jennifer Grey

City Centre, Winter

She clutches his elbow to cross the ice floe of the pavement
While shoppers become airborne between Tesco and New Look,
Arms stretched wide as if sufficient air resistance could arrest
Their slipslod dives. I track his passage through the flock,
Following the spoor of mud she left clung to the kerb.

Above us, the rain's been caught while making its escape:
Its afterimage dangled from the gutters indicates
The trajectory it could have taken on a different day.
As I reach to grasp his shoulder I find myself suspended,
Action interrupted inches from meaning what it should.

....

Jennifer Grey is the recipient of the 2013 Ink Sweat & Tears Poetry Writing Scholarship. She has been published both in print and online, and runs a series of poetry slams in the Norwich area. Her most recent projects include working with Writers' Centre Norwich on their 26 for Norwich collection.

Meghan Guss

Poet Lovers
Sinkhole
The Oral Tradition
Launch
Drone

Poet Lovers

They not only smell good, they're a bouquet.
Their sweat is a passionate miasma,
a nectar, a syrup between the joints.
It is not a seduction, it is Zeus,

turned to a swan, taking Leda by force,
force turning to motion, potential and
kinetic, mechanical energy,
a cold fusion of pheromones. It is

not sex. It is a metaphor. There are
tongues on things, on their secret places, on
turns of phrases. They lick each other's ess-
ence for glue to bond, to meld into one,

to seal envelopes holding odes for one
another, for the gods of lovemaking.
They are body paragraphs expounding
the metaphysical exchange of ink,

not fluids, a fountain, a pen dipping
the tip for a sonnet. When they argue
they shout beyond each other to the trees
behind them that bend and sway to the breath

of God, or whatever. The trees are more
than just trees, they hold ripe pomegranates
heavy and bursting blood red juice on to
a glossy white unicorn, chained beneath

the boughs, corralled, surrounded by plants that
make women fertile. The unicorn is
a symbol for Christ; it is hunted down
with wit, seduced into the poet's lap

for slaughter. The plants reconcile love
and marriage, the poets pluck and pumice,
to create the muse, to craft dynasties
of images, and then a pregnancy

of pauses. They are pretty flowers; some
are distilled in goat's milk or mixed with ox
dung and treat gout, snakebites, baldness, breathing
problems. And yes, they can cure nausea.

Because between their poet thighs are rose
buds blossoming and quivering stamen,
pollen all over their faces, in their
mouths, swallowing it, breeding within them

little baby poems, the progeny,
the food for thoughts, concepts growing in their
minds, feeding on their vision, malignant,
trapped, written with a scalpel to the head.

Sinkhole

One minute a man is sleeping,
then the minute shifts
and drops
like a marble into a funnel
and descends, circling round
the empty bulb of the hourglass
beneath his bed, formed over
hundreds of years,
a trickle of material
from top
to bottom.

The slow void of the hour migrates
to the surface, to what's left
of surface, the marble minute spinning
down the neck. Then all is swallowed,
the bed, the clothes, the books, the man.

Now I sleep as if I too am suspended
over the shape of a voluptuous woman,
each vitamin and mineral burning out
space, the bulb of the hourglass hollowing,
until I dream of perfect circles,
of open mouths.

The Oral Tradition

Some things are better left unsaid
he said, he knows a thing or two,
about unsaid things. What,
I cannot say. I cannot say
why, either because why
leads to because, why, I don't know.
Where is this place of unsaid things?
Says who? Nobody will
tell me, I've said nothing,
nowhere. They say what is
said is forgotten, I remember
hearing once, I remember he said
things are better, left unsaid,
I would not know.

Launch

Every day I think too much,
feeling the thoughts inflate

into a clutter of balloons, perky
as a school of fish and tied to my wrist.

I put them to paper, to release them,
but before I find my pen they drift
into a tree, each death a firecracker.
I think harder – deliberations
rigid and lumbering, bloated zeppelins

in the sky, the big writing
blundering across, the message
heavy and hollow.

I think maybe one thought
may escape and dwindle

above the clouds, intelligence dangling from its tail.

Still, there is no telling
who it may reach, or even
what it says.

Drone

The machines are breathing.
Lights fizzle and click above us,

still working in the new night.
The Earth is humming.

There is no explanation.
An infernal didgeri circulates
a route for hundreds of hours,
seeking our special heat.

Low tones underscore every life
every death that's here, that's here

to come. When I was born
my father struck a tuning fork

upon his palm and held it to my ear;
the pitch perfect and permanent,

distinguished from noise. My mother held
a conch shell to my ear. I misheard

my blood as the buzz of everything
alive, following me.

It sounds like someone
is always mowing the lawn.

....

Meghan Guss graduated from the University of Northern Iowa with a Bachelor's in Music and English Education. She taught high school English at a public school in Brooklyn, New York, for five years. She moved to England to study for a Master of Arts in Creative Writing (poetry) at UEA.

Kim Lockwood

Sundowning
Sustain
The Thought
they were scared maybe the water will come up
LP
What to Eat in Springtime

Sundowning

She sets the mugs of tea on the kitchen worktop, both stirred and one brewing in its own pool of milk, and says *it's misty outside*, and yes, you check then agree, it's misty outside.

From a different spoon she dumps sugar into both mugs, the spoon clinking on the side.

Control is easier now you know that both wrists fit in one hand's grip and you're both so good at being domestic you can split the morning duties of tea and toast.

And perhaps there was a moment when you were provoked into taking instead of asking but asking itself becomes implicit after a certain point of permission is passed, and you're certain that point was passed.

Between two fingers, she plucks out a teabag and sucks in breath as the heat starts to catch on her skin.

You would like to find your own newness.

To dive in a confluence of rivers and wait for that instant of solitude or solidarity to hit in the water's cold.

To steep your hands in ash and bathe in floodlit dark until you are returned to that balance you tried to hold before, you could try to hold before.

You watch steam rise.

Balance might not be enough. You have this stillness now and still you see the urgency that surfaced between looks; how guilelessly you were both drawn into your counterparts.

Sustain

Prod of frost-rich moss,
brittle, shifting

under touch. Its crispness
softens in the warmth

of my hand, pools
soon absorbed. I press

my fingers together
and in this rough calyx

I want
this touch to remain,

for the feeling of cold
form undoing

to be recalled and relived
as live sensation –

my nerves to open
like crocuses

to let this be kept, real
as contact, sustained.

The Thought

My first thought
is that the thought is beyond classification.

It bats at the glass for entry,
flattened against the pane.

I will not turn my back on it and I will not let it in.

I hear a sprinkle of wings
and furred thorax

beat at the low-hanging bulb,
beat at the light like it's lilac:

I am still as a label.

All night, the thought scatters itself
on bookshelves, plinks again and again against the walls

until I am caught and diagrammed, pinned in living display
and the thought can rest on the spire of my bedpost,

pat my hair with its feet for a double-tap taste
and drink from my mouth like it's flowers.

they were scared maybe the water will come up

You felt it coming. Your house racketed like a train, dust clouded from the walls. You moved to higher ground and from higher ground you watch the horizon rise. It advances in blocks of white, brined grey on white. Reality has fixity. You are part of that fixity and neither you nor reality belong to this weakening and folding, this unfolding of lines and boundaries. Cars pass. It is too cold today to be this fluid. You see a building bloat and you hold its walls together with your eyes until it mixes with the concrete seams swelling in the tide. Finally there is sound, above this sound the warning sirens fire. You plunged into a swimming pool. The water was cool and solid and you were fluid, weightless and fluid. Sound folded around sound and the warning sirens didn't fire. Your body moved through waves like a wall, through resistance that was deliberate and slower than air. You dived for a brick, and everyone clapped and smiled although you could scarcely lift it once you breached the surface.

LP

Arm brooks no   argument gathers me
to the chest   breath jagging a stylus   skipping vinyl
grooves caging scores   into strings caught   by a bow   strike
a sound expelled   from the rib-lunge taken
for permission which can't be
bitten back as   one hand fixates
on my hip guided   as a tonearm   the other
presses silence   to my mouth we meet
in the jinx
of the long play   quiet
your body   between me
and the door
I've been compliant
and sequestered
but never quite
so much of either   both
at once   before

What to Eat in Springtime

peaches aren't in season
but, in a wheelchair
with the footplates
raised acutely
he holds his leg
holds the tourniquet
around his thigh
the white tourniquet
and looks straight ahead
and does not
look down
so you look down
for him
you see his leg
below the knee
for him
gored like a peach
bitten though
to its stone
its furred skin
where missed by teeth
hanging open over
those little sinews
of structure
you know resist then tear then part
but where this falls apart
is in the bone
the prong of bone
out from the flesh so straight

that the tumble of flesh
looks natural
and the bone
looks less than human
less than the bitten through peach
and you only have to see this –
his face is calm and so dull –
you can't imagine
feeling and the sound
and the smell, you think
blood has a smell, but for you
the blood is in
the air is in
the sweet tang of peaches.

....

Kim Lockwood is co-editor of the *Lung Jazz: Young British Poets for Oxfam* anthology. Her work also features in the Everyman's Library anthology, *Villanelles*. Following her Creative Writing Poetry MA, she will start a PhD on postmodern American poetry at UEA.

Jackie Martin

When Architects Hear Voices
Edward de Vere and the Baking Metaphor
Best Supporting Other
House On The Corner
The New Shame
Docker

When Architects Hear Voices

Forget the grid,
the dull efficiency of box;
refuse the sanctuary of corners.

Liberate the crowds
pressed in, pressed out each day,
by widening my girth.

Resist the will of rectangles
so sugar can be spun
inside an office without envy.

Let the people mingle without rank,
blunt each other's edges,
curve their spines to my embrace.

Confront the tyranny of walls
so those who enter may be tempted
towards kindness.

Sink me thigh-deep, make me round,
surprise the evening traffic
scribbling at my hips.

Edward de Vere and the Baking Metaphor

After the stargazer,
after the Queen silvered the air
and clapped her hands
for what de Vere considered twaddle,
he was rumped upon the poet's chair
an hour more,
forced to endure the silly plays
of men with feeble hearts,
the lines sucked clean as breakfast pullet.
How might the truth be told?

Ed strayed off to the kitchen
where the cook was making saffron buns,
greeted him fondly, bawdily,
and pondered for a while.

The grape can change a man within an hour. All drunks take issue with their masters: wisdom skids, allegiance slips upon the twisted muscle of the tongue. Best soak a withered version of the fruit to slowly swell the yield. No knives – a spoon alone will stir the mob before the fire is goaded. Sweeten spite with wit, make salty every lover's whisper and the crowds will bellow at the hunchback in his costume gourd, pelt tripe and cabbage at his royal arse.

Now, who'd dissemble for a purse,
accept the author's call
and let de Vere stay clean?
He heard that Shakespeare
sold his inky curlicues of 'S'
for less than catskin shoes,

though vain enough for velvet,
and would bluster with the balls of youth
when censors held his throat.

As long as Ed convinced himself
that this was common sense,
not cowardice,
there was no rub.

Best Supporting Other

They move from scene to scene,
preferring not to sit on
chairs with stencilled names
in case they are directing furniture,
and some old cupboard gets upset.
It happens.

Or maybe one tired raindrop
breaking for a script rewrite,
a retake of the leafy leap
is threatening to quit:
that's when these whisperers
can really show their craft,
coaxing a mattress
to be pounded one more time,
champagne to gush on cue,
rubbish to huddle.

Their gifts are unacclaimed,
although the skill of speaking Curtain
charms the subtlest shrug
from jittery material,
framing the heroine as she moves
to centre stage.

House On The Corner

Clay heads swing heavy, slow,
from flower basket hooks on every bay,
sentinels that sleep in gutter shadows
through arrival of the milk, the mail, the meter reader,
gone in seconds.
The house remains unburgled,
kids detour to stare, dogs yank.

She greets them without fail,
shed-bound, peg-mouthed, crust-mucking each winter,
listens to the shifts in point of view after a sudden squall,
her long-dead relatives
cast by an expert hand to keep her company,
finished with a lead-free glaze
then wiped with turpsy cloth to put the spiders off.

The New Shame

God's stall was always busy,
plenty else on either side to lick a lip for:
clever stuff with foreign names and guarantees,
a store of superstition.
But women had been buying shame for centuries,
and God maintained a steady trade
with His routine,
the bristling-up before a sale.

Some years ago, it's true that stock was getting hard to shift,
what with the suffragettes and later, all those tiny skirts,
but now it's Friday best and veils
and girls are snaking round the corner from His pitch,
demand so high that backstreet boys
have started making up the goods themselves,
versions of His classic
touted up and down the line.

Docker

There was also a scent you carried
ship to shore:
a cloud of softwood, hops and must
from grain and green bananas,
currants trickled from a broken crate,
a mix of cargo that a child could soon discover
in the fabric of your coat.

No peril, no cruel winds and never shanties,
nothing more adventurous than
pocketing a mango from the hold.
The day you cracked your head across the deck,
you ran my finger down a row of tidy stitches,
laughed at your own joke:
they were shipshape, you said.

....

Jackie Martin has a background in fine art, design and television graphics, which sits alongside a parallel career in physical therapy. Add a love for making and eating cakes to arrive at some of the recurrent themes that colour her poems – imagery, science and baking.

Kate Pannett

While They Talked
Bottom Drawer
The Wilson
Slides
Couple's Therapy
Changing
Leaving

While They Talked

On those visits she wandered the rooms,
slipping away from their Sunday afternoon
to take the curve of the front stairs
up and into the aunt's bedroom
where her palms caught the fibres
of the pink rayon eiderdown,
its feather pockets shaken out to reach
the marital symmetry
of headboard and pillows.
Then she would turn to adjust
the three-way mirror on the dressing table
which blocked the window with
endless reflections of a porcelain bucket
and that girl rattling hairpins in a green glass tray.

Bottom Drawer

Really they were married at the jumble sale,
standing in the queue, expectant at the door
before dropping 10p into a biscuit tin and entering
the hall. A pin-striped jacket from the gent's table,
traces of crimson lake in a flattened handbag
and tea at the hatch served with the smell of gas,
the women fussing over huge kettles.
She found a blue-and-white dinner plate,
crackle glazed from someone else's oven,
he said he'd take the typewriter and be a novelist.
They spent the afternoon dancing the wooden floor,
out to the tables, back to the centre, sharing
their special bargains before departing
with two empty suitcases and a rolled umbrella.

The Wilson

Before the car it was everything,
that pram – generous sixties relic
hung on leather straps,
big enough to build home in.
It bowled along on hooped wheels,
the cavernous hood umbrella taut,
our pavement felucca, a sail across
the windy ridge above the railway.
Then chase a roll down into town,
negotiate the market for green peppers,
onions in brown paper bags, loose apples
poked alongside a crumpled child.
Stowed beneath, a slither of library books,
washing powder and bags of flour,
more vehicle than baby carriage,
smooth white handle responsive to a touch
and budging up along the bench, the children
a barouche of dangling legs, toddler shoes
jostled with clenching fists, rocked with
sprung buoyancy ready for the big push home.

Slides

There is no snow,
just this shallow overspill
dropped into the afternoon,
frozen water meadow,
grass blades trapped beneath
a sheet of creaking slide.
Tentative, holding hands,
your sturdy first shoes
and our dusty rubber boots,
we take you forth to feel
that glassy no-grip thrill
sliding out, everything
slipping away.

Couple's Therapy

We crawl into the sweep of drive.
A gardener looks up
and too aware, we cross the gravel
clutching notes and key words
to remind us to tell her things, like students.
A shuffling wait on the quarry tiled porch,
logs piled for winter, a single bulb suspended above
and as the front door opens a bruised card
is hung on the brass knob, *engaged* in biro.

Seated in a triangle of chairs we watch the hearth,
a blue-and-white china basin, a rug with a crease,
and take turns to spew out our toads
spoiling the soft-furnishings with this private poison.
Beyond the window a broad curve of grass
follows windblown trees towards a climbing frame.

She has passed me tissues,
glanced at the clock
and now it's over.
We step through the polished hall
subdued light showing the way
and here we are emerging,
coming down the cracked concrete steps
out into a raking of leaves, half expecting confetti.

Changing

They slip down from the pink-washed houses
to meet with the early roll of the sea,
a plunge at the edge into private churning,
before breakfast, before clamour,
strokes pulling in the wave stretch
adrift with the tide until
with salt-swilled hair, flat to their skulls,
they fumble back up the drag of shingle
and wrap into a swirl of towels
dropping the stringy twists of costume,
breasts unleashed, rubbing to warm,
arms reaching into the beach air
women drying like washing.

Leaving

There is a cold shadow under the deckchair.

Wet towels pulled from a rope stiff with salt,

the slow trudge up the beach dragging spades,

channels and pebble homes scuffed over by departures.

A trace of grit in the bath.

....

Kate Pannett has worked as a theatrical costumier and studied English Literature in London. She now works as a primary school teacher in Norfolk and has a large extended family. She's had work in Smiths Knoll who nominated her poem *Knitting* for the 2012 Forward Prize.